FAITH, STRATEGY & EXECUTION

FAITH, STRATEGY & EXECUTION

Build the Business God Assigned to You

PREFACE

Why I Wrote This Guide

If you and I were sitting across from each other right now, maybe in a quiet corner of a café, maybe after a long meeting, or maybe on a day when the weight of your calling feels heavier than usual, this is exactly what I would tell you:

You are not called to build your business alone. God cares about your work more than you realize and the marketplace needs what he placed inside of you.

For more than sixteen years, I have advised entrepreneurs, start-ups, business owners, and visionaries across the Caribbean and the United States. I've sat with people in moments of breakthrough and in moments of deep discouragement. I've watched clients go from confusion to clarity, from fear to courage, from idea to impact.

And throughout every stage of my own journey, as a consultant, researcher, teacher, author, and believer, one truth has remained unshakably clear:

Faith is not separate from business.
Faith is the strategy behind every God-given assignment.

This book was born out of that conviction.

A Different Kind of Business Book

There are countless business books on strategy, leadership, marketing, innovation, and scaling. I have read them, taught them, and even written in that space myself.

But this book is different.

I did not write this as a textbook.
I did not write this as a sermon.
I did not write this as a distant instruction manual.

I wrote this as a conversation,
a dialogue between you and me,
between the entrepreneur and the mentor,
between the builder and the believer in you.

I wrote this for the moments you feel God calling you higher but fear pulling you back.
For the moments when strategy feels overwhelming and execution feels impossible.
For the moments you know you're gifted… but you're not sure you're ready.

This is the book I wish I had when I started my entrepreneurial journey.
This is the book many of my clients needed before we ever met.
This is the book the Holy Spirit kept pressing into my heart to write.

The Bible Is More Strategic Than Most Business Plans

Some people see Scripture as an inspirational text.
Entrepreneurs often treat it as a spiritual accessory.

But the Bible is full of:

- business models,
- economic principles,
- leadership frameworks,
- negotiation strategies,
- risk management,
- succession planning,
- team building,
- innovation insights, and
- stewardship mandates.

From Joseph's economic forecasting, to Nehemiah's project management, to the Proverbs entrepreneur, to Jesus' teachings on stewardship, the Word of God has always been a business manual for those willing to see it through the right lens.

This book exposes what has been there all along.

A Book for the Modern Christian Entrepreneur

You live in a world of:

- digital disruption,
- competitive markets,
- rapid change,
- increasing pressure,
- limited attention spans,

- conflicting advice, and
- overwhelming expectations.

You are navigating both market realities and spiritual responsibilities. This book honors both.

Inside these chapters, you'll find:

- biblical truth,
- practical strategy,
- modern business principles,
- personal reflection,
- leadership insights,
- spiritual encouragement,
- and a challenge to build boldly with God.

My goal was simple:
To equip you to become a Kingdom entrepreneur, faithful, strategic, disciplined, and courageous.

A Personal Invitation

As you turn each page, I want you to feel as if we're walking together.

I want you to hear my voice reminding you:

- You are capable.
- You are called.
- You are equipped.
- You are supported.
- You are needed.

And I want you to hear God's voice even louder saying:

- "Write the vision."
- "Be strong and courageous."
- "Commit your plans to the Lord."
- "Do not despise small beginnings."
- "I will be with you."

This is not just another business book. This is a guide for your assignment. A companion for your journey. A reminder that faith belongs in the marketplace, and so do you.

Welcome to Faith. Strategy. Execution.

We walk from here, together.

Dr. Jason C. Charles
KokiYaY Business Consulting LLC
Founder, Consultant, Mentor, Believer

INTRODUCTION

A Conversation That Could Change Everything

Before you go any further into this book, I want to tell you something clearly and sincerely:

You were not created to live a life of small thinking, small impact, or small purpose. There is something God placed inside you that the world needs. Your business is part of that calling.

This book is not just ideas on paper. It is a conversation, one we're about to have with honesty, depth, and intention.

Your journey as a Christian entrepreneur is not an accident. Your desire to build something meaningful is not a coincidence.
Your passion, frustration, ambition, and even your questions are clues to something bigger.

You are reading this because God is preparing you for your next level.

The Journey You're About to Take

This book is going to challenge you, not to become someone else, but to become the fullest version of who God created you to be.

Together, we will explore:

- Faith: your spiritual foundation, your anchor, your strength.

- Strategy: your plan, your clarity, your blueprint.

- Execution: your discipline, your consistency, your obedience.

This is the formula.
This is the path.
This is the transformation.

Business Is Spiritual: Whether You Realize It or Not

Many Christians underestimate how deeply spiritual entrepreneurship is.

Business involves:

- influence,
- decisions,
- stewardship,
- leadership,
- risk,
- purpose,
- people,
- resources,
- and impact.

These are not just practical realities, these are spiritual responsibilities.

Every invoice you send, every project you launch, every employee you lead, every customer you serve…
all of it is connected to something much bigger than profit.

The marketplace is one of the greatest mission fields on earth.

Your business is not outside of God's plan.
Your business *is* part of God's plan.

And nothing is more powerful than an entrepreneur who understands this.

How to Read This Book

Don't read this book quickly. Read it intentionally.

Pause when something speaks to you. Write down what the Holy Spirit impresses on your heart. Reflect on the questions. Take action on the assignments.

This book is meant to:

- strengthen your spirit,
- stretch your mindset,
- sharpen your strategy,
- and elevate your execution.

Treat this as mentorship in written form.

Let these pages walk with you through:

- early mornings,
- work challenges,
- difficult decisions,
- moments of doubt,
- and moments of breakthrough.

Dedicated to:

Onike, Niah, Emma-Lee, Aalyiah, Omari, Nathan, Josiah

Contents

CHAPTER 1

FAITH COMES FIRST: THE SPIRITUAL FOUNDATION OF DECISION-MAKING

Come, sit with me for a moment.

Before we talk strategy, business models, scaling, leadership, or the thousand decisions you make every week as an entrepreneur, we must talk about faith, not in a religious sense, but in the deeply practical way God intended it.

Because whether you realize it or not, faith is your first business tool.

You see, most people think business begins with an idea. But ideas can come from anywhere. Kingdom business begins with alignment. It begins with who you trust before you take your first step.

When Proverbs 16:3 says, *"Commit to the Lord whatever you do, and He will establish your plans,"* it is not offering poetic comfort. It's delivering a strategic order of operations:

Faith → Strategy → Execution.

Not the other way around.

Faith comes first because without it, strategy becomes guesswork, and execution becomes survival. But with faith? Strategy becomes revelation, and execution becomes obedience.

And obedience always produces results.

1

The Marketplace Belongs to God

Entrepreneurs often carry unnecessary pressure.
We behave as though the entire world of business rests on our shoulders, as though we must personally manufacture clients, create opportunities, and make doors open by sheer force of effort.

But Psalm 24:1 interrupts that thinking:
"The earth is the Lord's, and everything in it."

Everything means:

- Markets
- Money
- Opportunities
- Contracts
- Customers
- Resources
- Networks
- Timing
- Favor

You are not fighting for space in a competitive world. You are operating inside a marketplace God created and still manages. That alone should lift the anxiety from your chest.

Faith as a Strategic Advantage

Let's be honest, you already know what fear feels like. You know what doubt sounds like. You know the pressure of leading a business, a vision, or a dream when resources feel limited, when competition looks stronger, or when the future feels unclear.

But what most Christian entrepreneurs forget is this:

Faith is not just spiritual strength. It is strategic intelligence.

Faith allows you to:

- Make decisions without panic
- See opportunities others overlook
- Trust timing others doubt
- Lead with clarity rather than confusion
- Move boldly because God already moved ahead of you

Faith sharpens your instincts because the Holy Spirit is the greatest advisor you will ever have.

In consulting, I have seen brilliant entrepreneurs fail because fear suffocated their creativity, or because impatience rushed their strategy. I have also seen average ideas succeed because the leader had the courage and humility to follow God's timing.

As Christians, we are not called to be naïve or unprepared. We are called to be spiritually guided and strategically equipped.

The Battle Between Fear and Calling

Every entrepreneur has two voices competing inside them:

1. The voice of calling — pulling you toward purpose.
2. The voice of fear — pulling you back toward safety.

Most entrepreneurs think they lack resources.
But more often, what they lack is courage.

Fear says:

- "You don't have enough capital."
- "You're not ready."
- "You might fail."
- "People will criticize you."
- "This is too risky."

Calling says:

- "Walk by faith, not by sight."
- "I am with you."
- "Start with what you have."
- "Do not despise small beginnings."
- "Be strong and courageous."

The truth is simple but uncomfortable:

You cannot follow fear and follow God at the same time. If fear is leading your decisions, faith isn't. If faith isn't leading your decisions, you will always hesitate at the threshold of your destiny.

God as the Ultimate CEO

Think of your business as a partnership. A divine joint venture.

You may be the founder, but God is the CEO.

God has:

- A better view of the market
- Infinite understanding of timing
- Perfect knowledge of your gifts
- Foreknowledge of risks
- Access to opportunities you cannot see
- A plan for your growth and transformation

4

When James 1:5 says, *"If any of you lacks wisdom, you should ask God,"* it is not referring to academic wisdom. It is talking about decision-making power, clarity in uncertainty, strategy in chaos, and insight when logic alone cannot guide you.

Your competitive advantage in the marketplace is not hustle.

It is heaven's guidance applied to earthly work.

Faith Moves You Before the Evidence Appears

Business is full of unknowns.
Markets shift.
Clients hesitate.
Plans change.
Competition arises unexpectedly.

But faith trains you to move without needing guarantees.

Hebrews 11:1 defines faith as
"confidence in what we hope for and assurance about what we do not see."

Meaning:

Faith is not blind.
Faith sees differently.

Faith looks at:

- A small idea and sees a national business.
- A single client and sees a scalable model.
- A small beginning and sees future impact.
- A slow season and sees preparation.
- Delays and sees protection.

Faith becomes the lens through which strategy becomes bold and execution becomes consistent.

Without faith, uncertainty feels threatening.
With faith, uncertainty feels like an invitation.

A Personal Word, From Me to You

Let's pause here.

Close the business plans.
Forget the projections.
Ignore the noise of comparison.
Put aside the anxiety you've been carrying.

Let me ask you something directly:

> What would you do if you were not afraid?
> What would you build?
> What would you launch?
> What conversation would you have?
> What idea would you start executing today?

The answer to that question often reveals your calling.

Fear limits.
Calling releases.

You are not reading this book by accident. God is preparing you for something deeper, stronger, and more purposeful than just profit.

Your business is not simply a career choice.
It is an assignment.

Your First Assignment of the Book

I want you to take a moment after this chapter and ask God a simple but powerful question:

"Lord, what have you already told me to do that I have not yet done?"

Then write down the first thought that comes to your heart.

That is where faith begins.
That is where strategy takes shape.
That is where execution becomes obedience.

Closing Thought

Entrepreneurship without faith is exhausting.
Entrepreneurship with faith is transformative.

Your journey does not start with a business plan.
It starts with trust.

Faith is your foundation.
Faith is your first strategy.
Faith is your fuel for execution.

Welcome to the journey.
Let's walk this out, together, with God leading.

Assignment 1 - *I want you to take a moment after this chapter and ask God a simple but powerful question:*

"Lord, what have you already told me to do that I have not yet done?"

_____

_____

_____

_____

_____

_____

_____

_____

_____

_____

_____

_____

_____

_____

_____

_____

_____

_____

_____

_____

_____

_____

_____

_____

CHAPTER 2

VISION & STRATEGY: WHAT IT REALLY MEANS TO WRITE THE VISION

Take a breath.
Settle your thoughts.
Let's talk about the one thing every entrepreneur claims to have, but few actually understand:

Vision.

Vision is one of the most misused words in business. Many entrepreneurs think vision is simply "what you want your business to become." But Scripture teaches something deeper, something far more demanding, and far more powerful.

Habakkuk 2:2 tells us:

"Write the vision and make it plain on tablets, so that a runner may run with it."

This is not a suggestion.
This is a three-part strategic instruction:

1. Receive the vision
2. Document the vision
3. Execute the vision

Vision is not just imagination...
Vision is assignment.
Vision is responsibility.
Vision is stewardship.

And if faith is your foundation, vision is your direction.

Vision Begins With God, Not You

In business, people often say:

- "Follow your passion."
- "Chase your dreams."
- "Do what you love."

But Scripture rarely instructs someone to follow themselves. Instead, it points us toward God's intentions.

Your vision is not merely a reflection of your preference.
It is a revelation of your purpose.

There is a difference between a personal dream and a divine assignment.

A personal dream says:
"This is what I want."

A divine assignment says:
"This is what God entrusts me to build."

One is born from ambition.
The other is born from obedience.

And here is the truth most entrepreneurs eventually discover:

The vision God gives you will always be bigger than what you believe you can do alone.

Why?
Because God designs vision to require dependence, discipline, and partnership, with Him and with others.

The Vision God Gives Requires Clarity

"Write the vision and make it plain."

Plain means:

- Clear
- Specific
- Measurable
- Actionable
- Understandable
- Transferable

If your team can't understand it, they can't run with it.
If your family can't understand it, they can't support it.
If you can't articulate it, you can't execute it.

The greatest threat to vision is not opposition—it's vagueness.

A vague vision creates:

- Scattered effort
- Confusion
- Wasted energy
- Burnout
- Doubt
- Misalignment

A clear vision creates:

- Focus
- Motivation
- Strategic direction
- Unity
- Progress

- Confidence

Clarity is not optional.
Clarity is strategic obedience.

Vision Without Strategy is Wishful Thinking

Let's talk practically, entrepreneur to entrepreneur.

Most people stop at writing the vision.
They don't make it plain.
They don't build a strategy.
They don't create the systems.
They don't align their actions.

They "write the vision" and then wait to be inspired.

But God does not bless vague desires.
He blesses disciplined stewardship.

Vision is not enough.
You need strategic structure.

A God-given vision requires:

- A plan
- A model
- A structure
- A timeline
- A pathway
- A sequence

Planning is not a lack of faith.
Planning is evidence of it.

Noah didn't build the ark by "trusting God and seeing what happens."
He followed blueprints.
Dimensions.
Measurements.
Systems.
Timelines.

Faith instructed him.
Strategy sustained him.
Execution validated him.

That is the blueprint for every Kingdom entrepreneur.

A Vision Not Written is a Vision Not Real

I want to say something to you directly:

If your vision is still floating in your head,
it is not a vision,
it is a hope.

Vision becomes real when it becomes visible.

Write it.
Map it.
Plan it.
Structure it.
Develop it.
Evaluate it.
Present it.
Test it.
Refine it.

This is how vision becomes strategy.

The moment you write the vision, you make a declaration: "I am preparing my life for what God revealed."

Strategy Bridges Faith and Execution

Let's define strategy simply:

Strategy is the system that carries your vision to reality.

Your vision is *what* God asked you to build.
Your strategy is *how* you will build it.
Your execution is *when* you actually act.

Faith informs vision.
Vision informs strategy.
Strategy informs execution.

Execution reveals obedience.

This is why you can't skip strategy.
Faith without strategy produces inconsistency.
Strategy without faith produces pride.
Execution without strategy produces chaos.

All three must work as one.

OUR VISION CLARITY FRAMEWORK™

1. Faith Alignment

What has God revealed, confirmed, or impressed on your heart about this assignment?

2. Purpose Definition

Who is the business called to serve? Why does it exist?

3. Strategic Direction

What are the measurable outcomes God expects you to pursue?

4. Market Reality

What resources, opportunities, competitors, and gaps exist?

5. Operational Pathway

What steps, systems, skills, and structures will make the vision executable?

You Cannot Run With What You Have Not Written

The end of *Habakkuk 2:2* says:

"...so that a runner may run with it."

This means:

- Vision creates momentum.
- Vision accelerates progress.
- Vision produces movement.

If you feel stuck...
If you feel delayed...
If you feel unclear...

It is likely that your vision is not written plainly enough.

Most entrepreneurs do not suffer from lack of opportunity. They suffer from lack of clarity.

Clarity turns waiting into preparation.
Clarity turns confusion into direction.
Clarity turns ideas into impact.

A Personal Word, Let's Talk Honestly

Let me ask you a direct question:

When was the last time you actually wrote your vision?

> Not typed a note on your phone.
> Not memorized it.
> Not talked about it.
> Not pitched it.

> Wrote it.
> On paper.
> With intention.
> With detail.
> With focus.
> With faith.

Written vision is accountable.
Written vision is measurable.
Written vision is transferable.
Written vision is trackable.
Written vision is prayer-worthy.

Unwritten vision is optional.
Written vision becomes a commitment.

CHAPTER 2 Assignment

Before you move to the next chapter, I want you to write down:

1. What God told you to build
2. Who you are called to serve
3. What success looks like over the next 12 months

Don't overthink it.
Write what flows.
Clarity comes through writing.

Closing Thought

Vision is not what you see with your eyes.
Vision is what you see with your spirit.

Strategy is not what you hope will happen.
Strategy is what you intentionally design.

When you write the vision,
you honor the One who gave it.
You prepare the path for those who will walk with you.
You activate the discipline needed for execution.

This is the beginning of building your business God's way.

Let's keep walking
because the next chapter will show you the character required
to *carry* the vision God gave you.

Assignment 2 - I want you to write down:

What God told you to build
Who you are called to serve
What success looks like over the next 12 months

_____
_____
_____
_____
_____
_____
_____
_____
_____
_____
_____
_____
_____
_____
_____
_____
_____
_____
_____
_____
_____
_____
_____

CHAPTER 3

THE CHARACTER OF A KINGDOM ENTREPRENEUR

Pull your chair a little closer.

We've talked about faith.
We've talked about vision and strategy.
But there's something even more important, something God cares about more than your business plan, your projections, or your ambition.

Your character.

Before God elevates an entrepreneur,
He examines the heart of the entrepreneur.

Before He gives you influence,
He checks your integrity.

Before He expands your territory,
He strengthens your foundation.

Why?

Because your character is the container that holds your calling.
If the container is weak, the calling spills.
If the foundation is cracked, the business cannot stand.

You must become the kind of person who can carry what God wants to give you.

Your Character Is a Strategy

This may surprise you:

Character is not just spiritual, it is strategic.

When you are building a business, your character directly impacts:

- Your brand
- Your leadership
- Your decision-making
- Your culture
- Your partnerships
- Your reputation
- Your ability to withstand pressure
- Your long-term success

A Kingdom entrepreneur understands that character is not optional. It is operational.

Look at Daniel.
Look at Joseph.
Look at Nehemiah.

Their character opened doors no résumé ever could.
Their integrity preserved them through seasons of crisis.
Their discipline earned the trust of kings.

Your gifts may create opportunities,
but your character determines whether you can keep them.

The Four Pillars of Kingdom Character

Let's talk practically now, entrepreneur to entrepreneur.

There are four essential traits every Christian business leader must cultivate:

1. Integrity: Doing Right When It's Not Convenient

Integrity is the quiet strength of leadership.

It is not glamorous.
It is not loud.
It does not seek attention.

But it builds something far more valuable:

Trust.

Trust with clients.
Trust with employees.
Trust with partners.
Trust with God.

Proverbs 10:9 says,
"Whoever walks in integrity walks securely."

Security in business does not come from profits, policies, or popularity.
It comes from integrity.

If you are going to lead a business God can bless,
you cannot:

- Cut unethical corners
- Manipulate clients
- Overpromise and underdeliver
- Compromise your values
- Hide important details

- Chase money over principle

Integrity may slow you down temporarily,
but it accelerates you permanently.

2. Humility: The Posture of a Teachable Leader

Humility is misunderstood.

It is not weakness.
It is not silence.
It is not shrinking back.

Humility is right posture.

It is the openness to say:

- "I don't know everything."
- "I can learn from others."
- "God knows more about this business than I do."

Humility protects you from arrogance, poor decisions, and
blind spots.

Pride says:
"I've got this."

Humility says:
"God, guide me."

Pride makes decisions alone.
Humility invites wisdom.

Every great entrepreneur you've ever admired, whether
Christian or not, had this one trait:

They remained teachable.

No matter how high God takes you,
stay small enough for Him to continue shaping you.

3. Boldness: Courage Wrapped in Purpose

Courage is not the absence of fear.
Courage is moving while fear whispers.

A Kingdom entrepreneur must be bold, not reckless, not impulsive, but bold in purpose.

Boldness allowed:

- David to face Goliath
- Esther to confront the king
- Paul to preach to hostile cities
- Nehemiah to rebuild walls no one believed in
- Peter to step out on water

Your business will require uncomfortable decisions:

- Starting when you feel unprepared
- Launching with faith, not full certainty
- Saying no to the wrong opportunities
- Having difficult conversations
- Raising your standards
- Trusting God's timing over your timeline

Boldness is not a personality trait.
It is a spiritual decision.

When you move with God, you can move with confidence.

4. Stewardship: Managing What You Have as Preparation for What You Want

Stewardship is the discipline of responsibility.

God does not promote entrepreneurs who mismanage:

- Time
- Money
- Relationships
- Resources
- Opportunities
- Excellence
- Reputation

The parable of the talents (*Matthew 25*) is not about money. It is about stewardship leading to multiplication.

Notice this:
The servant who multiplied his talent did not get a *bigger opportunity*.
He got greater responsibility.

Entrepreneurs often pray:
"God, enlarge my territory."

But God asks:
"How have you stewarded the territory you already have?"

When stewardship is high, growth becomes natural.
When stewardship is low, growth becomes dangerous.

Leadership Is Not What You Do, It's Who You Are

Many business owners try to improve their leadership by improving their skills.

But biblical leadership begins with improving your heart.

The marketplace is full of:

- Talented people with poor character
- Gifted leaders with toxic attitudes
- Successful individuals with fragile integrity
- Visionaries who crumble under pressure

This book is for you because you are choosing a different path. You recognize that your greatest business investment is your personal development.
Not the motivational kind
the spiritual kind.

Before God grows your business, He grows you.

Pressure Reveals the Leader

Let's talk honestly.

Pressure will not only come… it must come.   Why?

Because pressure reveals:

- Your maturity
- Your consistency
- Your emotional discipline
- Your spiritual capacity
- Your leadership readiness

Pressure exposes cracks before they become collapses.

When God allows you to face difficult clients, financial strain, confusion, or obstacles, He is not sabotaging you, he is strengthening the places success will rest on.

Pressure is a divine diagnostic tool. It shows you what needs refinement.

Nehemiah: A Case Study in Leadership Character

Nehemiah was not a priest.
Not a prophet.
Not a king.
Not a general.

He was, interestingly, a government worker with a burden.

Yet his character positioned him to rebuild an entire nation's wall.

He demonstrated:

- Integrity: He would not be manipulated
- Humility: He sought wisdom and God's guidance
- Boldness: He stood firm against opposition
- Stewardship: He planned, measured, assigned, organized

Nehemiah is the model for the modern Christian entrepreneur facing:

- Limited resources
- Hostile environments
- Sabotage
- Fatigue
- Leadership pressure
- Discouraged teams

CHAPTER 3 Assignment

Before moving to the next chapter, reflect and write:

1. Where do I need more integrity?
2. In what areas must I become more teachable?
3. Where is God calling me to be bold?
4. What resources have I not stewarded well?

There is no shame in your answer, only direction.

God grows who He plans to use.

Closing Thought

Character is not built in a moment.
Character is built in decisions.

Decisions to honor God.
Decisions to lead with truth.
Decisions to stay humble.
Decisions to be courageous.
Decisions to steward your assignment well.

When your character is strong,
your vision is safe.
Your strategy is stable.
Your execution becomes sustainable.

You are not just building a business.
You are becoming a leader God can trust with influence.

Assignment 3 - Reflect and write:

1. Where do I need more integrity?
2. In what areas must I become more teachable?
3. Where is God calling me to be bold?
4. What resources have I not stewarded well?

_____
_____
_____
_____
_____
_____
_____
_____
_____
_____
_____
_____
_____
_____
_____
_____
_____
_____
_____
_____
_____
_____

CHAPTER 4

RISK, INNOVATION & COURAGE: FAITH IN THE UNKNOWN

Take a deep breath.
This is the chapter where many entrepreneurs either rise… or retreat.

Let's talk about risk, the kind that feels uncomfortable, stretches your faith, challenges your logic, and forces you to trust God in ways you've never had to before.

Let's talk about innovation, the creative power God placed inside you to solve problems the world hasn't solved yet.

And let's talk about courage, not the absence of fear, but the decision to move even while fear whispers.

Because if you're going to be a Kingdom entrepreneur in today's world, you will need all three.

Faith Is Not Safe

Some Christians mistakenly believe that faith means comfort. Faith is not comfortable, faith is courageous.

Almost every biblical assignment required someone to step into the unknown:

- Abraham left without knowing the destination.
- Moses walked into Pharaoh's court with only a staff.
- David faced a giant with a slingshot.
- Joshua crossed the Jordan at flood stage.
- Peter stepped out of a boat in a storm.

God has a consistent pattern:
He calls His people into environments where they must trust
Him.

If you feel stretched, uncertain, and challenged, don't panic.
It means you're on the right track.

Risk Is Not Reckless: It Is Required

Let's define a Kingdom understanding of risk:

Risk is the willingness to move without having every answer
because you trust the One who does.

The world defines risk as danger.
Scripture defines risk as obedience.

The world says,
"Wait for guarantees."

God says,
"Walk by faith."

The world asks,
"What if it doesn't work?"

Faith asks,
"What if God is in this?"

When God gives you an assignment, the greater risk is not
stepping out
the greater risk is disobedience.

Fear Paralyzes, Faith Mobilizes

Let me speak to you directly.

Fear will always try to negotiate with your destiny.

Fear will say:

- "This is not the right time."
- "You don't have the money."
- "People will laugh."
- "You might fail."
- "What will others think?"
- "Play it safe."

But faith says:

- "Move now."
- "Start with what you have."
- "God is with you."
- "This is your moment."
- "Be bold."

Fear is persuasive.
Fear is logical.
Fear is loud.

But fear is also a liar.

Faith does not silence fear, it simply refuses to obey it.

Innovation: Creativity as a Spiritual Assignment

Innovation is not just a modern business concept.
Innovation is biblical.

Look closely at Scripture:

- God gave Noah blueprints no one had ever seen.
- Joseph introduced a national economic strategy that saved nations.
- Bezalel (*Exodus 31*) received divine creativity to design the tabernacle.
- Solomon built infrastructures that were architecturally unmatched.
- Paul innovated a missionary system that shaped the world.

Innovation is the expression of God's creativity through human stewardship.

When you innovate, you are not being "extra." You are being obedient to the creative DNA God placed in you.

Innovation is not about chasing trends. Innovation is about solving problems with God-inspired insight.

The Enemy of Innovation Is the Comfort Zone

Comfort is the place where ideas die.
Comfort destroys potential.

Comfort whispers:

- "Do it the way it has always been done."
- "Don't try something new."
- "Don't disrupt the familiar."
- "Stay safe."

But all growth requires discomfort.

If your business feels too familiar, too predictable, too easy, it may be a sign you are no longer growing, you are maintaining.

Maintenance is not multiplication.
Maintenance is not kingdom impact.
Maintenance is not obedience.

God didn't call you to maintain.
He called you to innovate.

Peter & the Boat: The Blueprint for Courage

Let's revisit the famous moment in *Matthew 14*: Peter walking on water.

Peter *was not walking on water.*
Peter was walking on the Word.

Jesus said,
"Come."

That was the strategy.
Everything else was execution.

Peter stepped out in faith.
He began something impossible.
Then he looked at the wind.
He saw waves.
Fear entered.
He started sinking.

This moment teaches us something profound:

You sink when you stop looking at God and start looking at conditions.

The waves were always there.
The storm never went away.
But as long as Peter kept his eyes on Jesus, the impossible became his new normal.

Entrepreneurship is the same:
If you stare at your bank account, you'll sink.
If you stare at competitors, you'll sink.
If you stare at failure statistics, you'll sink.
If you stare at uncertain markets, you'll sink.

But if you stare at the One who called you...
you will rise above conditions others drown in.

Your Assignment Will Always Require More Than Comfort

God will never call you to something that only requires your strengths.
He will call you to something that requires your faith.

Why?

Because when the results come,
only God can get the glory.

If you could do it alone,
you wouldn't need Him.

This is why He pushes you into unfamiliar territory:

- new markets
- new products
- new ideas
- new platforms
- new partnerships
- new levels of leadership

He wants to expand you before He expands your business.

Courage Is a Daily Decision

You don't become courageous once.
You choose courage every day.

Every time you:

- pitch your business
- invest in yourself
- make a difficult decision
- set boundaries
- start something new
- trust God in uncertainty
- innovate boldly
- take the next step

...you are choosing courage.

Courage does not eliminate fear.
Courage outruns it.

Faith-Based Risk Management (A Practical Framework)

FAITH-BASED RISK MODEL™

1. *Revelation Risk:*
   What did God tell you, show you, or confirm?

2. *Strategic Risk:*
   What are the measurable factors (market, timing, resources)?

3. *Capacity Risk:*
   Do you have the skills, discipline, and team for this step?

4. *Obedience Risk:*
   What happens if you *don't* move?

5. *Kingdom Impact:*
   Who benefits if you succeed? Who suffers if you delay?

Let's Talk Honestly: A Personal Word

Tell me, what are you afraid of right now?

Be honest with yourself.

Is it:

- failure?
- embarrassment?
- financial risk?
- what people will think?
- stepping outside your comfort zone?
- losing something safe?
- making the wrong decision?

Whatever it is, I want to tell you something with all sincerity:

Fear is trying to talk you out of what God already approved.

Fear wants you to stay where you are.
Faith wants you to step into who you are becoming.

You cannot build a God-sized vision with human-sized comfort.

CHAPTER 4 Assignment

Before moving to the next chapter, write down:

1. What risk is God asking me to take right now?
2. Where am I resisting innovation?
3. What would I start today if I trusted God fully?

Let these answers guide your strategy.

Closing Thought

Faith doesn't guarantee predictability.
Faith guarantees guidance.

When you embrace the discomfort of risk,
the discipline of innovation,
and the decision of courage,

you become the kind of entrepreneur who can walk in places
others only dream of.

You don't need perfect conditions.
You don't need all the answers.
You don't need every doubt removed.

You need one thing:

Obedience to the God who called you.

The next chapter will show you how leadership, rooted in love,
wisdom, and purpose, shapes teams, culture, and influence.

Assignment 4 - Reflect and write:

1. What risk is God asking me to take right now?
2. Where am I resisting innovation?
3. What would I start today if I trusted God fully?

_____
_____
_____
_____
_____
_____

_____
_____
_____
_____
_____
_____

_____
_____
_____
_____
_____
_____

_____
_____
_____
_____
_____

CHAPTER 5

PEOPLE, LEADERSHIP & CULTURE: BUILDING TEAMS GOD CAN BLESS

Lean in for this one.

Because if your business is going to grow, if your vision is going to expand, and if your assignment is going to impact people beyond yourself, you must understand something fundamental:

God blesses people… and people build businesses.

You cannot fulfill a God-sized vision alone.
Not because you are incapable,
but because God designed Kingdom work to require community, unity, and collaboration.

Even Jesus, God in the flesh, chose a team.

That should tell you something.

Leadership Is Ministry

Some entrepreneurs see leadership as a position.
But Kingdom entrepreneurs understand leadership as ministry.

Leadership is not about:

- your title,
- your authority,
- your position,
- your cleverness,

- or the size of your organization.

Leadership is about service.

Jesus said in *Matthew 20:26*:
"Whoever wants to become great among you must be your servant."

The world leads from power.
Kingdom leaders lead from purpose.

The world commands.
Kingdom leaders influence.

The world demands loyalty.
Kingdom leaders earn trust.

Leadership is not what you do to people—
Leadership is what you build inside people.

Your Team Is Your Stewardship

Many entrepreneurs pray for:

- growth,
- expansion,
- new customers,
- higher revenue,
- organizational breakthrough.

But God often responds with something far less glamorous:

"Take care of the people I gave you."

Your employees, contractors, partners, and supporters are not just part of your business.
They are part of your stewardship.

Your team is not there to simply fulfill your vision.
You are also called to contribute to *their* purpose.

A Kingdom business is not just a workplace.
It is a development ground.

Culture is Not an Accident, It Is a Creation

Every workplace has a culture.
Healthy cultures are formed intentionally.
Toxic cultures form by neglect.

Culture is:

- How people feel at work
- What behavior is tolerated
- What values are enforced
- How communication flows
- How decisions are made
- What is celebrated
- What is unacceptable
- How people grow

If you don't build culture, culture will build itself.
And self-built culture tends to drift toward dysfunction.

You shape culture through:

- your behavior
- your tone
- your consistency
- your integrity
- your decisions
- your expectations
- your systems

- your consequences

Culture is leadership made visible.

Nehemiah: A Blueprint for Team Leadership

Return for a moment to Nehemiah, one of Scripture's greatest organizational leaders.

He did not rebuild the wall by himself.
He built an engaged, motivated, aligned workforce.

Nehemiah led with:

- Prayer
- Planning
- Assignment clarity
- Accountability
- Vision repetition
- Encouragement
- Expectation of excellence
- Conflict management

And here's the key:
His team believed in the vision because they believed in his character.

Teams do not follow titles.
Teams follow trust.

Three Types of People God Sends to Your Business

As a Christian entrepreneur, you will encounter three categories of people:

1. Builders

These are your Nehemiah partners—
people who help build the vision with loyalty, excellence, and enthusiasm.

They:

- take initiative
- solve problems
- add value
- carry the weight with you
- protect the culture
- grow with the company

Builders are a blessing.
When God sends them, honor them.

2. Consumers

These are people who take from the business but do not contribute meaningfully.

They:

- drain energy
- resist growth
- complain more than they contribute
- undermine culture
- depend on others to carry them

Consumers are not evil—they are simply misaligned.
Your job is to discern whether they need development... or
release.

3. Disrupters

These are people the enemy sends to destabilize culture,
derail vision, or introduce confusion.

They:

- gossip
- resist authority
- sow division
- challenge values
- undermine unity

Do not fear disrupters.
Do not entertain them.
Do not negotiate with them.

A Kingdom entrepreneur protects their culture like a shepherd
protects a flock.

Leadership Requires Emotional Intelligence

Let's talk practically.

Leadership doesn't just require vision.
It requires emotional maturity; the ability to:

- stay calm under pressure
- listen actively
- communicate clearly
- set boundaries

- correct with grace
- encourage generously
- make decisions without emotional impulsiveness

A leader who cannot manage their emotions
soon cannot manage their team.

Emotional intelligence is not weakness, it is wisdom.

Delegation: Your Leadership Stretch

If you want your business to grow, you cannot do everything.

Let me say that again, firmly and kindly:

You. Cannot. Do. Everything.

Delegation is not losing control.
Delegation is expanding capacity.

Moses learned this when Jethro told him to appoint leaders
who could share the responsibility (Exodus 18).
When Moses stopped trying to do everything alone, the nation
flourished.

Delegation frees you to:

- think strategically
- build systems
- innovate
- rest
- mentor
- grow
- steward your assignment

The inability to delegate is not a skills issue.
It is a trust issue.

Trust God.
Trust the people He sends.
Trust the process of leadership.

Correcting Without Crushing

Correction is necessary in leadership, but the Kingdom entrepreneur does not correct to shame; they correct to strengthen.

Paul instructed Timothy to correct with gentleness and clarity.

Corrections should:

- be specific
- be respectful
- focus on behavior, not identity
- offer a path forward
- reinforce your values
- protect dignity

If people fear your correction, they hide problems.
If people trust your correction, they grow through it.

Creating a Culture God Can Bless

A culture God blesses reflects the fruits of the Spirit:

- love
- joy
- peace
- patience
- kindness
- goodness

- faithfulness
- gentleness
- self-control

A business led by these values becomes a place where:

- excellence is natural
- unity is strong
- conflict is resolved quickly
- creativity thrives
- burnout is reduced
- morale is high
- purpose is felt
- God is honored

When God sees a culture that reflects His nature, He sends people, resources, and opportunities that match that culture.

CHAPTER 5 Assignment

Before you move on, reflect on these three questions:

1. What culture am I unintentionally creating?
2. Who on my team is a builder, consumer, or disrupter?
3. How can I become a more Christ-centered leader this month?

Write it down.
Pray over it.
Take action.

Closing Thought

A Kingdom entrepreneur does not just build a business.
They build people.
They build systems.
They build culture.
They build spaces where God's character can be seen.

Leadership is not about being in charge.
Leadership is about being responsible
for the people, the environment, and the vision entrusted to you.

When you lead well, your team thrives.
When your team thrives, your business grows.
When your business grows, God's glory expands.

In the next chapter, we explore something every entrepreneur faces: finances, stewardship, and scaling; God's blueprint for multiplication.

Assignment 5 - Reflect and write:

1. What culture am I unintentionally creating?
2. Who on my team is a builder, consumer, or disrupter?
3. How can I become a more Christ-centered leader this month?

_____

_____

_____

_____

_____

_____

_____

_____

_____

_____

_____

_____

_____

_____

_____

_____

_____

_____

_____

_____

_____

_____

_____

CHAPTER 6

FINANCES, STEWARDSHIP & SCALING:
MULTIPLYING WHAT GOD PUTS IN YOUR HANDS

Let's settle into this one with intention.

Because if faith is your foundation, and vision is your
direction, and character is your anchor,
stewardship is how you convert God-given potential into God-
honoring results.

Finances are not just numbers.
Finances are a test.
Finances are a tool.
Finances are a responsibility.
Finances are fuel for the assignment.

And scaling is not simply growth,
it is *multiplication*.
It is stewardship elevated.

This chapter is about learning how to manage what God
places in your hands in a way that positions you for increase.

The Parable of the Talents: The Blueprint for Multiplication

Let's begin with the most entrepreneurial chapter in Scripture:
Matthew 25.

A master gives three servants money to manage:

- One receives 5 talents
- One receives 2

- One receives 1

They receive *according to their ability*, meaning God never gives you more than you can handle, but he fully expects you to grow what He gives you.

Two of the servants invest, multiply, and return with more. The master celebrates them:
"Well done, good and faithful servant... You have been faithful over little; I will set you over much."

But the third servant buries the money out of fear and returns it unchanged.

The master calls him:

- wicked,
- lazy,
- unfaithful,
- and lacking stewardship.

This parable is not about money.
It is about faithfulness, responsibility, strategy, and courage.

In Kingdom entrepreneurship:

- Faithfulness leads to increase
- Fear leads to stagnation
- Obedience leads to opportunity
- Stewardship leads to scaling

You cannot pray for multiplication while practicing maintenance.

Stewardship Is Not Management, It Is Multiplication

Most people think stewardship means "being careful."
But biblical stewardship is not conservative, it's productive.

Stewardship involves:

- growing what you have,
- using what you have,
- improving what you have,
- expanding what you have,
- investing what you have,
- and multiplying what you have.

God does not reward preservation.
God rewards multiplication.

Preservation says:
"I must protect what I have."

Stewardship says:
"I must multiply what God entrusted to me."

You Are Not the Owner, You Are the Steward

Psalm 24:1 says:
"The earth is the Lord's, and everything in it."

Everything includes:

- your business
- your income
- your team
- your opportunities
- your clients
- your resources
- your networks
- your gifts

You don't own the business.
You manage it on God's behalf.

This mindset shifts everything:
You steward with humility.
You scale with courage.
You spend with wisdom.
You invest with purpose.
You earn with integrity.

A Kingdom entrepreneur never asks,
"What do I want to do with my business?"
The real question is,
"What does God want to do through this business?"

Financial Discipline Creates Spiritual Capacity

Many Christian entrepreneurs pray for financial increase while practicing financial disorder.

God will not pour abundance into a leaking vessel.

Financial stewardship requires:

- Budgeting
- Tracking expenses
- Honoring commitments
- Reducing waste
- Managing debt wisely
- Knowing your numbers
- Creating margins
- Setting aside reserves
- Planning for taxes
- Separating business and personal finances

Financial discipline is not unspiritual; it is obedience.

You cannot multiply what you do not manage.

Cash Flow Is the Lifeblood of Your Business

Profit is your score.
Cash flow is your survival.

Even highly profitable businesses fail due to poor cash flow management.

You need:

- predictable cash inflows
- controlled expenses
- payment terms that protect your business
- pricing that reflects your value
- regular financial reviews
- systems, not guesswork

Cash flow is not a financial issue, it is a strategic one.

Scaling Requires Systems, Not Stress

Scaling is not simply "getting bigger."
Scaling is growing in a way that:

- maintains excellence
- protects culture
- increases capacity
- expands impact
- supports sustainability

Too many entrepreneurs scale emotionally instead of strategically:

- They hire too fast
- Add services they can't support
- Expand without structure
- Chase growth without systems
- Overextend financially

That is not scaling.
That is self-sabotage.

Scaling requires:

- clear processes
- automation
- delegation
- consistent quality
- financial readiness
- stable leadership
- a healthy culture
- strong accountability

Growth without structure becomes failure at scale.

The Multiplication Mandate: God Expects Increase

Genesis 1:28 is the first instruction ever given to humanity:
"Be fruitful and multiply."

This was not about children alone, it was a mandate for
expansion, productivity, dominion, creativity, and stewardship.

Multiplication is not optional. Multiplication is biblical.

God expects you to:

- grow personally
- grow spiritually

- grow financially
- grow organizationally
- grow impactfully

If your business has stayed the same for years, something needs to be revisited:

- vision
- leadership
- systems
- faith
- or stewardship.

God never calls us to stagnation.
He calls us to stewardship—
and stewardship always produces multiplication.

The Four Levels of Financial Stewardship

1. Survival Stewardship

Managing just enough to stay afloat.
Reactive. Unpredictable. Stress-driven.

2. Stability Stewardship

Bills paid, systems improving, small margins forming.
Predictable. Organized. Disciplined.

3. Strategic Stewardship

Using financial insight to make strategic decisions.
Intentional. Scalable. Vision-aligned.

4. Multiplication Stewardship

Investing, expanding, automating, reinvesting, and multiplying profits.
Kingdom-impact driven. Growth-focused. Legacy-building.

Most entrepreneurs never move past level 2.
Your goal is level 4.

Scaling Requires Letting Go of Small Thinking

Small thinking says:
"Just enough for me."

Kingdom thinking says:
"Enough to bless, employ, serve, expand, and impact."

Small thinking says:
"I don't want to grow too much."

Kingdom thinking says:
"I want everything God desires for me to steward."

Small thinking says:
"Let me play safe."

Kingdom thinking says:
"Let me play obedient."

Your business is not meant to stay small if God designed it to influence many.

Your Relationship With Money Must Be Healed

Some Christian entrepreneurs secretly fear money, avoid money, or mismanage money because they misunderstand money.

You must reconcile these truths:

- Money is not evil.
- The love of money is the problem.
- Money is a tool.
- Money is a test.
- Money is a responsibility.
- Money reveals maturity.

You cannot demonize what God is trying to multiply.

Wealth in the right hands becomes Kingdom influence.

CHAPTER 6 Assignment

Before you move to the next chapter, complete these three steps:

1. Evaluate your stewardship level:

Survival?
Stability?
Strategic?
Multiplication?

2. Identify one area of financial discipline that must improve:

Cash flow?
Budgeting?
Pricing?
Tracking?
Debt?
Unexpected expenses?

3. Identify one area where God is calling you to scale:

A service?
A product?
Your team?
Your systems?
Your reach?

This is not theory, this is obedience.

Closing Thought

God is not looking for perfect entrepreneurs.
He is looking for faithful stewards.

When you manage well, God multiplies.
When you steward well, God expands.
When you honor God financially, He honors your business.

You are not building for survival.
You are building for Kingdom impact.

And the God who gave you the vision
will give you the increase
when He can trust you with the stewardship.

Assignment 6 - Reflect and write:

_____
_____
_____
_____
_____
_____
_____
_____
_____
_____
_____
_____
_____
_____
_____
_____
_____
_____
_____
_____
_____
_____
_____
_____
_____
_____
_____
_____
_____

CHAPTER 7

EXCELLENCE & EXECUTION; DOING THE WORK GOD ASSIGNED

Let's have an honest conversation.

You have faith.
You have vision.
You have strategy.
You have character.
You're learning stewardship.
You're developing leadership.

But none of that matters if you don't execute.

Execution is where obedience becomes visible.
Execution is where prayers turn into progress.
Execution is where God's instructions meet your discipline.

Most entrepreneurs don't fail because of lack of ideas.
They fail because of lack of follow-through.

Execution is the bridge between potential and results.

Faith Without Works Is Dead, So Is Vision Without Execution

James 2:17 makes a powerful statement:

"Faith by itself, if it is not accompanied by action, is dead."

Now let's adapt this for entrepreneurs:

Vision by itself, if it is not accompanied by execution, is useless.

It sounds harsh, but it's truth wrapped in love.

God did not give you a vision
so you could admire it.
God gave you a vision
so you could *build* it.

Execution is not optional.
Execution is obedience.

God Blesses What You *Do*, Not Just What You *Intend*

Intentions are beautiful.
But God blesses work.

Noah built the ark plank by plank.
David practiced his sling before he killed Goliath.
Ruth worked in the fields before she stepped into destiny.
Paul traveled from town to town preaching tirelessly.
Jesus worked the ministry daily, teaching, healing, discipling.

Miracles are supernatural.
Execution is practical.

A Kingdom entrepreneur embraces both.

Excellence Is Not Perfection, It's Stewardship

Let's clarify something:

Excellence is not being flawless.
Excellence is honoring God with your best.

Colossians 3:23 says:
"Whatever you do, work at it with all your heart, as working for
the Lord…"

Excellence means:

- you prepare well
- you refine your craft
- you honor timelines
- you communicate clearly
- you show maturity in your work
- you deliver quality consistently
- you build systems that sustain results

Excellence is a message.
It tells the world:
"I represent the Kingdom, so I cannot offer anything careless."

Discipline: The Secret Ingredient of Execution

You cannot build consistently without discipline.

Many entrepreneurs ask for motivation.
But motivation is a mood.
Discipline is a decision.

Discipline does not ask:
"How do I feel today?"

Discipline asks:
"What needs to be done today?"

Discipline is the muscle that carries your assignment.

Without discipline:

- tasks pile up
- consistency disappears
- excellence fades
- opportunities slip

- clients lose confidence
- your vision stagnates

God will give you strength, wisdom, and support—
but *discipline* is something you must choose.

Execute Even When You Don't Feel Inspired

Let me free you from a lie many creatives and entrepreneurs
believe:

You will not always feel inspired.

But you must still execute.

Inspiration is seasonal.
Consistency is spiritual.
Impact is cumulative.

Some days execution looks like breakthroughs.
Some days it looks like routines.
Some days it's detail work no one sees.
Some days it's hard.
Some days it's ordinary.
But all of it is progress.

Kingdom builders do not wait for inspiration.
They work from conviction.

Distractions Are the Enemy of Execution

Where there is destiny, there will always be distraction.

Common distractions include:

- social media scrolling

- comparison
- busywork instead of meaningful work
- procrastination
- overthinking
- fear of failure
- perfectionism
- unnecessary meetings
- emotional exhaustion

Not all distractions are sinful.
Some are simply misaligned.

The enemy doesn't need to destroy your vision.
He just needs to distract you from building it.

The Power of Systems & Routines

Execution becomes easier when it becomes predictable.

Systems protect:

- your time
- your focus
- your energy
- your excellence
- your momentum

A Kingdom entrepreneur needs:

- morning routines
- weekly planning rhythms
- monthly reviews
- quarterly strategy check-ins
- automated systems
- documented processes

- consistently scheduled work blocks

Systems turn obedience into lifestyle.

Momentum: The Hidden Force Behind Execution

Momentum is spiritual and practical.

Momentum means:

- small steps compound
- consistency becomes easier
- wins begin to multiply
- productivity increases naturally
- confidence grows
- opportunities accelerate

You don't need to make giant leaps.
You just need to take consistent steps.

Momentum is built on discipline.
Momentum is fueled by excellence.
Momentum is protected by focus.

Slowing Down Is Not Quitting

Let me gently say this:

Rest is not laziness.
Rest is obedience.

God instituted Sabbath for a reason.
Your body has limits.
Your mind has limits.
Your emotions have limits.

Rest restores creativity.
Rest resets discipline.
Rest revives clarity.

Burnout is not a badge of honor.
It is a warning sign of misalignment.

A rested entrepreneur executes better.

Your Calling Requires Both Prayer *and* Productivity

Prayer without execution leads to stagnation.
Execution without prayer leads to burnout.

Prayer gives direction.
Execution gives results.

God wants you to do both.

Pray.
Plan.
Execute.
Repeat.

This is the rhythm of Kingdom entrepreneurship.

A Personal Word, Let's Be Honest Together

Let me ask you the most important question of this chapter:

What has God told you to do that you have delayed?

Is it:

- launching something?
- finishing something?

- fixing something?
- rebuilding something?
- stopping something?
- investing in something?
- becoming disciplined in something?
- hiring someone?
- saying no to something?

Delayed obedience is disobedience.
And delayed execution delays blessing.

You already know what needs to be done.
God isn't waiting to speak
He's waiting for you to move.

CHAPTER 7 Assignment

Before moving forward, write these down:

1. One thing you will execute THIS WEEK.

Not tomorrow.
Not "soon."
This week.

2. One area where excellence must improve.

Communication?
Work quality?
Client experience?
Timeliness?

3. One distraction you will eliminate.

Social media?
A habit?
A relationship?
A fear?
A thought pattern?

Commit to action.
Your future self will thank you.

Closing Thought

Execution is where faith becomes visible.
Execution is where obedience becomes fruit.
Execution is where God multiplies effort and rewards diligence.

When you work with excellence,
God breathes on your work.

When you discipline yourself,
God expands your capacity.

When you execute consistently,
God establishes your success.

You are not just dreaming anymore.
You are building.
You are becoming.
You are executing the assignment Heaven entrusted to you.

Next, we move into one of the most necessary and overlooked realities of entrepreneurship:

Assignment 7 - Reflect and write:

_____
_____
_____
_____
_____
_____
_____
_____
_____
_____
_____
_____
_____
_____
_____
_____
_____
_____
_____
_____
_____
_____
_____
_____
_____
_____
_____
_____
_____

CHAPTER 8

BATTLES, SETBACKS & SPIRITUAL WARFARE; WINNING THE INVISIBLE FIGHT

Come closer for this one.

Because I want to speak to a part of entrepreneurship many people never talk about openly.
Something you've felt but maybe never had words for.
Something that explains why some seasons feel harder than they should.
Something that reveals why progress often attracts resistance.

Here is the truth:

Every Kingdom assignment comes with opposition.
Every God-given vision will be challenged.
Every entrepreneur doing God's work will face spiritual warfare.

Not the Hollywood kind.
Not the dramatic, exaggerated kind.

But the quiet, strategic, relentless pressure that tries to wear you down, distract you, and discourage you.

You are not imagining the resistance.
You are not "too sensitive."
You are not weak.

You are in a spiritual battle.

And this chapter will show you how to win.

You Have an Enemy Because You Have an Assignment

The enemy does not attack those doing nothing.
He attacks those building something.

He attacks:

- vision
- peace
- confidence
- clarity
- finances
- relationships
- momentum
- purpose

Why?
Because if he can stop the builder, he can stop the building.

This is not to make you fearful
it is to make you aware.

The moment you said "yes" to God's assignment,
you stepped onto a battlefield.

But hear me:

The enemy may challenge you,
but he cannot defeat what God has ordained.

Nehemiah: A Masterclass in Overcoming Opposition

Nehemiah's calling was clear: rebuild the wall.
But immediately, opposition came.

Sanballat and Tobiah mocked him.
They ridiculed the vision.
They questioned his motives.
They tried to discourage him.
They tried to distract him.
They tried to intimidate him.
They threatened violence.
They tried to stop the work completely.

Here is Nehemiah's response:
He prayed… and kept building.

He didn't come down from the wall.
He didn't argue.
He didn't quit.
He didn't get distracted.
He didn't lose focus.

He said,
"I am doing a great work and I cannot come down."
—Nehemiah 6:3

That is your posture too.

How Spiritual Warfare Shows Up in Entrepreneurship

You may not see demons with pitchforks, but warfare appears
subtly through:

1. Discouragement

The sinking feeling that makes you question everything.

2. Delay

Opportunities slow down.
Progress feels stuck.
Doors seem closed.

3. Distraction

Everything suddenly competes for your attention.
You lose focus.
Your energy gets scattered.

4. Division

Team conflicts arise.
Misunderstandings occur.
People become difficult.

5. Doubt

"Did I really hear God?"
"Is this worth it?"
"Did I make a mistake?"

6. Fatigue and Burnout

You feel drained.
Unusually tired.
Mentally foggy.

7. Financial Attacks

Unexpected bills
Clients who delay payments
Sudden shortages

8. Fear and Anxiety

You feel pressure that doesn't match the situation.

These are not coincidences.
They are coordinated attempts to break your spirit before you finish your assignment.

The Goal of Spiritual Warfare Is Not to Destroy You; It Is to Stop You

The enemy knows something you may not fully grasp yet:

If you complete your God-given assignment,
people will be blessed,
lives will be changed,
families will be impacted,
doors will open,
and God's Kingdom will expand.

So the enemy aims for something simpler:

Stop you from building.
Stop you from executing.
Stop you from trusting.
Stop you from moving.
Stop you from showing up.

That's why the battle is so fierce.
Your obedience is dangerous to darkness.

You Must Learn to Fight Spiritually and Strategically

You are not just a business owner
You are a spiritual architect.

And architects must learn to battle on two fronts:

1. The spiritual realm (through prayer, Scripture, worship, fasting)

and

2. The natural realm (through discipline, planning, leadership, wisdom)

Nehemiah held a sword in one hand
and a tool in the other.

This is the posture of a Kingdom entrepreneur.

Your Spiritual Weapons

Paul says in *Ephesians 6:12*:

"We wrestle not against flesh and blood..."

Your real enemy isn't:

- competitors
- clients
- critics
- coworkers
- family members
- other entrepreneurs

Your battle is spiritual.

And God has equipped you with weapons that actually work:

1. Prayer

Your most powerful strategy meeting.
Nothing changes atmosphere like prayer.

2. The Word of God

Your offensive weapon.
Speak Scripture over your business daily.

3. Worship

Worship breaks heaviness.
It resets your spirit and silences fear.

4. Fasting

Sharpens discernment.
Strengthens resolve.
Re-aligns your priorities.

5. Community

You need people who can pray with you and hold you
accountable.

These weapons are not symbolic
they are effective.

Use them.

Setbacks Are Part of the Assignment: Not Proof of Failure

Let me tell you something crucial:

A setback is not a sign that you made a mistake.
A setback is often confirmation you are on the right path.

Joseph went from pit → prison → palace.
David went from oil → obscurity → opposition → kingship.
Paul went from revelation → persecution → revival.

Every biblical leader faced setbacks
on the way
to destiny.

Not instead of destiny.
On the way to destiny.

Your setbacks are not punishment.
They are preparation.

Discouragement Is Not a Signal to Quit, But to Pray

Sometimes spiritual warfare shows up as emotional heaviness.
A weight on your chest.
A tiredness of the soul.

This is not weakness.
This is warfare.

Psalm 61:2 says:
"When my heart is overwhelmed, lead me to the Rock that is higher than I."

When discouragement comes:

- Go to God
- Go to the Word
- Go to worship
- Go to prayer
- Go to purpose

Do not go to fear.
Do not go to comparison.
Do not go to self-pity.

Discouragement is a spiritual attack on your perspective.
Do not let it rewrite your calling.

CHAPTER 8 Assignment

Before you continue, do this:

1. Identify the battle you're currently facing.

Write it down. Name it.

2. Identify the lies the enemy is trying to tell you.

Replace each lie with Scripture.

3. Pray this simple prayer:

"Lord, strengthen my hands for the work.
Silence every voice that is not Yours.
And help me to finish what You started."

Closing Thought

The presence of warfare does not mean you are losing.
It means you are advancing.

The enemy is fighting because your vision is dangerous.
Your assignment is valuable.
Your obedience is powerful.

But here is the truth:

What God has ordained, no attack can overturn.
What God has blessed, no enemy can curse.
What God has begun in you, He will complete.

Stand firm.
Keep building.
Keep praying.
Keep trusting.
Keep executing.   Your victory is already written.

Assignment 8 - Reflect and write:

_____

_____

_____

_____

_____

_____

_____

_____

_____

_____

_____

_____

_____

_____

_____

_____

_____

_____

_____

_____

_____

_____

_____

_____

_____

_____

_____

_____

_____

_____

CHAPTER 9

PURPOSE, LEGACY & IMPACT: BUILDING WHAT OUTLIVES YOU

Come a little closer
this chapter is personal.

Because at some point in your entrepreneurial journey, you
will realize something profound:

Success is not enough.
Impact is what your soul is truly after.

Money is good.
Growth is exciting.
Opportunities are rewarding.

But none of these compare to something deeper:

Living out your God-given purpose
and leaving behind something that outlives your time on earth.

This chapter is not about building big businesses.
It's about building meaningful ones.

Purpose Is the Why Behind Your Work

Purpose is not the same as profit.
Purpose is not the same as passion.
Purpose is not the same as recognition.

Purpose is the reason God placed this assignment inside you.

Purpose answers:

- *Why does my business exist?*
- *Who is it called to serve?*
- *What problem am I uniquely called to solve?*
- *What transformation am I meant to bring?*

Purpose is not chosen.
Purpose is revealed.

You don't invent your purpose.
You discover it.

And once you discover it, you can never go back to simply "running a business."
You start building a mission.

Your Business Is a Ministry

I want you to hear this clearly:

A Kingdom business is not secular work—
it is ministry disguised as entrepreneurship.

Your ministry is not always behind a pulpit.
It may be:

- in a conference room,
- in a board meeting,
- on a job site,
- in product design,
- in a consulting office,
- in an online platform,
- or in solving problems others avoid.

Every invoice you send,
every customer you serve,

every system you build,
every employee you develop…..   This is ministry.

Kingdom entrepreneurs minister through:

- excellence
- integrity
- service
- wisdom
- generosity
- influence
- leadership
- love

You may be the only expression of Christ some people ever see.

You preach through your work.

Legacy Is What Continues When You Stop Working

Legacy has nothing to do with age.
Legacy has everything to do with intention.

Legacy is:

- the systems you leave behind
- the people you developed
- the values you instilled
- the impact you created
- the communities you strengthened
- the opportunities you opened
- the wisdom you documented
- the lives you changed
- the story your business tells long after you're gone

Your business is temporary.
Your legacy is eternal.

Three Layers of Legacy

Below is a framework you can use in your mentoring,
consulting, and speaking—something unique to your voice:

1. Personal Legacy

Who you become through the journey.
Your character.
Your obedience.
Your faithfulness.
Your transformation.

2. People Legacy

How you influence and develop others.
The team you trained.
The leaders you raised.
The families you impacted.
The clients you empowered.

3. Kingdom Legacy

How your obedience expands God's work.
The prayers you prayed.
The seeds you sowed.
The spiritual deposits you made.
The purpose you fulfilled.

Most entrepreneurs focus on personal success.
Kingdom entrepreneurs focus on multi-layered legacy.

Impact: The Real Measure of Success

Success asks:
"What did I achieve?"

Impact asks:
"Who did I change?"

Success is visible.
Impact is eternal.

Success is what you build.
Impact is who you build.

Success is measured in profit.
Impact is measured in people.

Success is celebrated on earth.
Impact is rewarded in Heaven.

Don't just build a successful business.
Build one that transforms people.

Multiplication Through People

God's favorite strategy for expanding impact is simple:

He multiplies through people.

Think of it:

- Jesus invested in 12 men and changed the entire world.

- Paul mentored Timothy and ignited generational ministry.

- Moses raised Joshua.

- Elijah raised Elisha.

Everyone with Kingdom impact raises someone else.

Who are you raising?
Who are you mentoring?
Who are you developing?
Who will carry forward the work after you?

If your business dies when you stop working,
you built a job.
If it thrives beyond you,
you built a legacy.

Your Purpose Will Outlive Your Profits

Profits end when business ends.
Purpose continues long after.

Your purpose is the thread that connects:

- your calling
- your work
- your influence
- your future
- your legacy

Purpose keeps you grounded during success
and anchored during struggle.

Purpose makes strategy meaningful
and execution sustainable.

Purpose makes leadership intentional
and growth impactful.

You were not born to run a business.
You were born to fulfill a calling.

The business is the vehicle,
not the destination.

The Enemy Fights Purpose More Than Anything Else

Do you know why you face spiritual warfare?

Because purpose is dangerous.

Purpose:

- disrupts darkness
- influences people
- exposes deception
- elevates communities
- strengthens families
- shifts environments
- changes futures

Purpose is powerful
which is why the enemy tries to frustrate, distract, confuse,
and discourage you.

He fears what you carry.
He fears what you are building.
He fears the people you will impact.

But here is the truth:

Purpose cannot be stopped.
It can only be delayed by disobedience.

And you are not disobedient.
You are growing, learning, building, and becoming.

Your Business Must Become a Seed

Jesus said in *John 12:24*:

"Unless a grain of wheat falls to the ground and dies, it remains alone.
But if it dies, it produces much fruit."

Some things in your business must die for legacy to live:

- fear
- pride
- procrastination
- people-pleasing
- small thinking
- unnecessary control
- old systems
- outdated structures

When you let certain things die,
your business multiplies.

CHAPTER 9 Assignment

Before moving forward, reflect on and write the following:

1. My life purpose in one sentence:

(Pray before writing.)

2. The people I am called to impact:

Be specific.

3. One thing I must change today to build a lasting legacy:

Focus on action.

4. One person I will intentionally mentor or pour into this year:

Legacy multiplies through people.

Closing Thought

You are not building for applause.
You are building for impact.

You are not building for now.
You are building for generations.

You are not building for your name.
You are building for God's glory.

Your legacy will not be measured by income statements—
but by the lives touched because you obeyed your calling.

Your purpose is bigger than you.
Your vision is bigger than your lifetime.
Your impact is eternal.

Assignment 9 - Reflect and write:

_____
_____
_____
_____
_____
_____
_____
_____
_____
_____
_____
_____
_____
_____
_____
_____
_____
_____
_____
_____
_____
_____
_____
_____
_____
_____
_____
_____
_____
_____

CHAPTER 10

FAITH. STRATEGY. EXECUTION. YOUR FINAL ASSIGNMENT

This is our last conversation in these pages.

You've walked with me through faith, vision, character,
courage, stewardship, leadership, and purpose.
You've reflected.
You've prayed.
You've been challenged.
You've been stretched.
You've been strengthened.

Now there is only one thing left to do:

Decide.

Because everything you've read in this book comes down to
one essential truth:

God has already given you an assignment.
Now you must choose to walk it out.

No one can do that for you.
Not a mentor.
Not a pastor.
Not a friend.
Not even a book.

Obedience is personal.

This is your moment.
This is your invitation.
This is your commissioning.

Let's talk plainly
not author to reader,
but entrepreneur to entrepreneur,
believer to believer.

You Already Have What You Need

Some entrepreneurs wait for the perfect moment.
Others wait for clarity.
Some wait for confidence.
Some wait for confirmation.
Some wait for resources.

But God rarely waits.

He calls you *as you are*
with what you have
from where you stand.

Every major biblical assignment began in an imperfect
moment:

- Moses was insecure.
- Gideon was afraid.
- David was overlooked.
- Esther was unprepared.
- Peter was impulsive.
- Paul had a past.

Yet each one said yes,
and God did the rest.

The question is not,
"Do you have everything you need?"

The real question is,
"Will you trust God with what you already have?"

Faith Is Your Foundation

Faith is not the absence of fear.
It is the refusal to let fear lead.

Faith is not confidence in yourself.
It is confidence in the One who called you.

Faith is not naivety.
It is partnership.

Faith is the lens through which you see possibility where
others see impossibility, strategy where others see confusion,
and purpose where others see struggle.

Faith sees the invisible.
Faith believes the impossible.
Faith obeys the unreasonable.

If faith does not lead you,
your fears will.

Make your choice.

Strategy Is Your Blueprint

God gives vision.
But He also gives strategy.

Strategy is holy.
Planning is obedience.
Preparation is worship.

"Write the vision," He said.
"Make it plain."

That is not poetry.
That is instruction.

Strategy turns prayer into planning.
Strategy turns dreams into decisions.
Strategy turns vision into structure.

Strategy is the system that carries purpose to completion.

Do not insult your own calling by refusing to plan for it.

If God gave you the vision,
He expects you to develop the strategy.

Execution Is Your Proof

This is the part where many entrepreneurs fail.

Not because they lack:

- faith,
- ideas,
- passion,

- or calling…

…but because they lack consistency.

Execution is not glamorous.
Execution is not emotional.
Execution is not convenient.

Execution is obedience in motion.

Execution is saying:
"I will build, even when it's hard.
I will show up, even when I don't feel it.
I will finish what God told me to start."

Great visions die of neglect, not opposition.

It doesn't matter how inspired you are if you don't execute.

Execution is your worship.
Execution is your offering.
Execution is your demonstration that you believe God's
promise enough to act on it.

There Will Never Be a Perfect Moment

Stop waiting for certainty.
Stop waiting for applause.
Stop waiting for more money.
Stop waiting for more support.
Stop waiting to "feel ready."

You are not waiting on God—
God is waiting on you.

Every delay has cost you something:

- momentum
- impact
- influence
- opportunities
- personal growth
- spiritual maturity

This book was not written to inspire you temporarily.
It was written to activate you permanently.

You have enough clarity to begin.
You have enough direction to execute.
You have enough confirmation to obey.

Move.

Your Assignment Is Bigger Than You Realize

Your business is not just a source of income.
It is a source of influence.

Your work is not just a job.
It is a ministry.

Your vision is not just a dream.
It is a Kingdom solution.

People you have never met
are waiting for what God placed inside you.

Your obedience will affect:

- families,

- communities,
- employees,
- future leaders,
- ministries,
- and generations.

Purpose ripples.
Legacy multiplies.
Impact extends.

You do not build alone.
Heaven builds with you.

A Final Word: From My Heart to Yours

You made it to the final chapter.
That alone tells me something profound:

You are serious about your calling.
You are ready for more.
You are positioned for impact.

Before this moment fades into the busyness of life,
I want you to pause and reflect on one question:

What is God asking you to do NEXT?

Not someday.
Not eventually.
Not when the timing feels better.

Next.

Listen for the whisper.
It's already in your spirit.

Your Final Assignment

Write down your next three steps.

Not goals.
Not dreams.
Steps.

Actionable.
Specific.
Immediate.

STEP 1: What will you execute in the next 48 hours?

(This builds momentum.)

STEP 2: What will you execute in the next 7 days?

(This builds consistency.)

STEP 3: What will you execute in the next 30 days?

(This builds transformation.)

Then pray this prayer aloud:

"Lord, I commit my faith to You.
I commit my strategy to You.
I commit my execution to You.
Strengthen my hands for the work ahead.
Guide my decisions.
Protect my mind.
Expand my influence.
And let everything I build bring glory to Your name."

Amen.

Assignment 10 (The Final Assignment)- Reflect and write:

_____
_____
_____
_____
_____
_____
_____
_____
_____
_____
_____
_____
_____
_____
_____
_____
_____
_____
_____
_____
_____
_____
_____
_____
_____
_____
_____
_____
_____
_____
_____

www.ingramcontent.com/pod-product-compliance
Lightning Source LLC
Chambersburg PA
CBHW070456130626
46555CB00003B/1026